I0154160

John Coleman Adams

The fatherhood of God

John Coleman Adams

The fatherhood of God

ISBN/EAN: 9783337373979

Printed in Europe, USA, Canada, Australia, Japan

Cover: Foto ©Lupo / pixelio.de

More available books at **www.hansebooks.com**

Manuals of Faith and Duty.

No. I.

THE

FATHERHOOD OF GOD.

BY

REV. JOHN COLEMAN ADAMS, D.D.

"OUR FATHER WHO ART IN HEAVEN."

THIRD EDITION.

BOSTON:

UNIVERSALIST PUBLISHING HOUSE.

1890.

Copyright, 1888,

By the Universalist Publishing House.

University Press:

John Wilson and Son, Cambridge.

CONTENTS.

———◆———

SECTION   PAGE

I. RELATION OF THE DOCTRINE TO REVELATION   6

II. THE OLD TESTAMENT TEACHING   7

III. THE DOCTRINE OF OUR LORD   11

IV. THE APOSTOLIC DOCTRINE. 18

V. THE DOCTRINE OF ADOPTION   25

VI. THE TEACHING OF THE FATHERS   32

VII. DIVINE FATHERHOOD AND DIVINE LOVE   . . 38

VIII. FATHERHOOD AND HUMAN DEPRAVITY   . . . 51

IX. FATHERHOOD AND THE PROBLEM OF EVIL   . 57

X. FATHERHOOD AND RETRIBUTION   64

XI. THE DIVINE FATHERHOOD AND HUMAN
SORROW   74

XII. DIVINE FATHERHOOD AND HUMAN DESTINY   . 83

XIII. THE DIVINE FATHERHOOD AND HUMAN
CONDUCT   91

The best name by which we can think
of God is Father. It is a loving, sweet,
heart-touching name; for the name of Father
is, in its nature, full of inborn sweetness
and comfort.

MARTIN LUTHER.

THE FATHERHOOD OF GOD.

———◆◆◆———

"THE fatherly relation and purpose of God toward men," said Thomas Erskine, "is the fundamental revelation of Christianity." In that sentence, the spiritually-minded Scot announced the growing faith of his own day and of ours. This great fact of the Divine economy is the corner-stone of the Christian system. It was the end and aim of the unfolding revelation which God made to the nation to whom He committed the truth concerning His nature and His disposition. It is a truth which was perceived with a growing clearness as the work of revelation proceeded; and the inspiring idea in the mind of Him in whom that work culminated, is the fatherhood of God and man's sonship to Him. All the truths which Jesus Christ gave to man have their root in this fundamental truth; all the Saviour's teaching rests at last upon this

conception of God. And every fact of Christ's
dealings with men is tinged with a reflection
caught from the brightness of this radiant verity
of the spiritual universe.

I. — RELATION OF THE DOCTRINE TO REVELATION.

In saying that the truth of the Divine fatherhood was gradually made known to men, we but
follow the teaching which the most distinguished
and trustworthy defenders of the faith assert.
The course of revelation was progressive. There
is a steady advance in the announcement of
Divine truth, from the earliest statements of the
law, down to the universal principles made known
by Jesus Christ. As Dr. George P. Fisher says:
" It is plain that the religious consciousness, or
the general type of religious ideas and feelings,
rises higher and higher as we pass from one
epoch to another of Hebrew history. Only by
degrees did that which was latent in the relation
assumed by God toward men, come to the light.
. . . That Christianity is a higher stage in the
process of revelation, the New Testament leaves
us no room for doubt." [1]   Or as Canon Row says:

[1] Beginnings of Christianity, pp. 7, 9.

" Christianity . . . is a plant which has grown in a succession of gradual stages until its culmination in Jesus Christ."[1] Hence we shall not look for the same clear grasp of the fact in the minds of the Old Testament writers that we shall find in the souls of those on whom inspiration had fallen in later days.   Nevertheless, the Old Testament does certainly contain assertions of the nature of God's relation to man and man's relation to God, which serve as the lower courses in the rising structure of revealed truth, uncontradicted by later disclosures.

II. — THE OLD TESTAMENT TEACHING.

This fact gives great significance to the passages in the Old Testament which touch upon this relation of the Creator to humanity.   The record of the creation is couched in the phrase which colors all Christian thought. " Let us make man in our image, after our own likeness. . . . So God created man in His own image."[2] In what this likeness or image consists, we may discuss farther on ; but it is to be noted at this point that the illumination

[1] Bampton Lectures, 1877, p. 3.   [2] Genesis i. 26, 27.

which was sufficient to reveal this relation of
God to man was not enough to stamp it with
the name of fatherhood. The fact on which
that relationship rests was discerned, but not
the real nature of the bond between the Creator
and the creature. That was to await the coming
of a clearer vision.

But whatever may have been the nature of
this image and likeness of God, it is clear that
it was not lost in the sin of our progenitor,
inasmuch as in a later age, long after the pri-
meval sin, long after the curse was pronounced
against it, it was made the ground of the Divine
denouncement of murder. " Whoso sheddeth
man's blood, by man shall his blood be shed;
for in the image of God made He man." [1] It
is impossible to evade the force of this passage. It can have no meaning whatever except
upon the assumption that the image of God still
persists in the human soul, making a human life
a sacred thing, retaining, even though corrupt
and fallen, the essential nature in which the
race was formed. That single passage is fatal
to all that false view of human nature which
has tinctured the anthropology of the Christian

[1] Genesis ix. 6.

Church for fourteen hundred years. It is an impregnable text, standing between the truth of man's perpetual kinship to God by virtue of the Divine image in which he subsists, and the assaults of those who would declare him a spiritual orphan.

The same must be said of another word out of the mouth of the great law-giver of Israel. It is one of those rare and occasional utterances of the earlier men of God, which go to show that the idea of the universal fatherhood was struggling through the darkness of their time, — a foregleam of the fuller revelation yet to come. In the song of Moses he uses these remarkable words, "Do ye thus requite the Lord, O foolish people and unwise? is not He thy father that hath bought thee? hath He not made thee and established thee?"[1] This is not an address to saints, nor to those who by their devotion had secured the right to any special claim of sonship; for in the very verse preceding Moses has called those at whom this inquiry is aimed, "a perverse and crooked generation."

And in the same tone does Isaiah, speaking in Jehovah's name, say, "Hear, O heavens, and give

[1] Deuteronomy xxxii. 6.

ear, O earth: for the Lord hath spoken. I have nourished and brought up children, and they have rebelled against me." [1] If that relationship was still perpetuated after years of rebellion, sinfulness, and spiritual alienation from God, and its recognition authorized, it would not seem to have been utterly sundered by the fall. Still further evidence of the growing sense of God's fatherhood appears in the words of the prophet Malachi, where he speaks for Jehovah to Israel, and says, " A son honoureth his father, and a servant his master: if then I be a father, where is mine honour? and if I be a master, where is my fear? saith the Lord of hosts unto you, O priests, that despise my name." [2] And there is an evidence of the connection in the minds of these later prophets of the fact of creation with the truth of God's universal fatherhood in that other passage from the book of Malachi: " Have we not all one Father? hath not one God created us?" [3] That is not said of regenerate men, but of those [4] who have not kept God's ways. And it shows beyond question that in the mind of this prophet the fatherhood of

---

[1] Isaiah i. 2.   [2] Malachi i. 6.
[3] Ibid. ii. 10.   [4] Ibid. 9.

God was coextensive with His creatorship over
souls.

III. — THE DOCTRINE OF OUR LORD.

But the thought of fatherhood is still germinal, and its development and application in all
its tender and beautiful phases was reserved for
a greater than this prophet.

  Dr. Geikie, in his Life of Christ, strikingly
reiterates the words quoted from Thomas Erskine in the beginning of this book, when he says
that in the Sermon on the Mount Jesus makes a
new era for man. " He rises above his age and
announces a common Father of all mankind,
and one spiritual ideal in resemblance to Him." [1]
And Dr. Phillips Brooks, in the Bohlen Lectures for 1879, on the " Influence of Jesus," pro-
nounces Christianity a personal force, behind
which there lies one great inspiring idea, namely, " The fatherhood of God and the childhood of
every man to Him. . . . To reassert the fatherhood and childhood as an unlost truth, and to
re-establish its power as the central fact of life ;
to tell men that they were, and make them act-
ually be the sons of God, — that was the purpose

[1] Life of Christ, ch. 37.

of the coming of Jesus and the shaping power of His life." [1] The Sermon on the Mount is filled with the idea of the fatherhood of God. It was addressed to a "multitude." It was the delivery of a law to humanity. It was the announcement of a new standard of conduct for all men. And to assert that the frequent references to God's fatherhood in that discourse mean no more than His fatherhood to the elect and regenerate is to say that the whole sermon is no more than an exhortation to those who have entered the kingdom of God, and is not to be applied to mankind at large; because the references to the fatherhood are so interwoven with the exhortations, that to limit the one is to restrict the other. And that construction the sermon will not bear.

It was a continuous exhortation to men as children of God that they be worthy of their Father. Through all its shining sentences there runs this golden thread. The fact of God's fatherhood, the relationship between man and his Maker is urged and repeated and dwelt upon as the ground of obedience, of sacrifice, of self-denial, or of devotion. The sonship of man is always the primary fact. The reason for doing

[1] Influence of Jesus, pp. 12, 14.

or not doing, for thought or for action, is always this, namely, that the man may be worthy of his origin, — a true son, and not a disloyal one, fulfilling his own nature and destiny. "Be ye therefore perfect," he says, "even as your Father is perfect." "Love your enemies," in order, it appears, "that ye may be the children of your Father which is in heaven." "Let your light so shine before men that they may glorify your Father." Is it needful to multiply quotations? The whole Sermon might be cited as teeming with the most explicit repetitions in various keys and many modulations of this recurrent phrase of Divine truth, which is all summed up in the prayer He put into the mouth of humanity, whose opening words are "Our Father."

That prayer has been by universal consent considered the prayer for all classes and conditions of men. It is the voice of human nature crying to its God. In the words of Dr. Plumptre, "It is true of all men. . . . Our right to use that name is no peculiar privilege of ours, but is shared by every member of the great family of God." [1] The venerable Dr. Mark Hopkins, commenting upon these words, remarks: "This term

[1] Handy Commentary, vol. i. p. 78.

I suppose He intended to authorize all men to use, and that in the use of it, with the full understanding of its import, there is implied that image of God in which man was created." [1] To try to limit the scope of that address, comprehending as it does the most sacred truth ever unfolded to the mind of man, is a perversion of the Scripture which is excusable only to the blindest prejudice.

It is indeed sometimes argued that one who from the heart can use this prayer is not an " alien," but a disciple; is penitent, is a seeker after God, and so, by anticipation, a child of God. But for hundreds of years the Augustinian theology has taught that no man is entitled to call God father who is not regenerate; for only regeneration can create the filial bond. But simply to be penitent is not to be restored. The inquirer is not a convert; discipleship is not regeneration. To meet the truth of God with such perverse trifling with terms of the deeper meaning is lamentable if done in ignorance; is culpable if done through premeditation to maintain a cause. For in those words the Saviour of mankind thrust in upon our

[1] Scriptural Idea of Man, p. 26.

spiritual consciousness the solemn truth that we are by our very natures the children of God, whose image we sully when we sin, whose grace we abuse, whose love we grieve, when we give our souls to evil.

Nor is this the only discourse of our Saviour's in which He lays upon the heart of man this sacred truth. The parable of the Prodigal Son has been called the gospel within the gospel, so thoroughly does it compress within itself the significance of the message of our Saviour. And nothing can be made of its touching story except the fatherly attitude of God to man, and the filial nature and relationship which not even transgression can rupture. The father loves that son even in his exile. The son is still a son, even in his degradation. What better type could we ask of man's relations to his Father, which not even sin can break nor the corruptions of an evil life annul? What finer phrase was ever devised to express the essential nature of repentance than these words: "And when he came to himself?" What clearer inculcation could we ask of the truth that as man is a son of God by no act of his own, so no act of his can ever cancel the relationship; but that even in his deepest

degradation he may think of the Heavenly Father
as his father?   What stronger appeal could we
make to sinful men to be worthy of their sonship, and to earn and accept the rejected place
to which they are entitled ?

Those are significant words, too, which Jesus
uses in addressing the woman of Samaria, who,
being only an alien as yet and a stranger even
to the circle of Jewish ideas, as well as a soiled
and unregulated nature, is yet told of " The
Father " in that broad and inclusive tone which
is evidently meant to make her feel that God is
her father, because He is the Father of all flesh.
" Jesus saith unto her, Woman, believe me, the
hour cometh when ye shall neither in this moun-
tain nor yet at Jerusalem worship the Father.
. . . The hour cometh and now is when the true
worshippers shall worship the Father in spirit
and in truth : for the Father seeketh such to
worship Him."   Here is a term used broadly,
as if in the Saviour's mind it represented an
established and universal relationship.   To limit
its meaning to a relation to the saved, would be
to make the term one of the most inappropriate
that could be used to this unconverted heathen.
The clear intent of our Lord was to make her

feel what she had in all likelihood never dreamed before, that the God to whom the varying worship of Samaritan and Jew was rendered was the common Father of both peoples, — " The Father " of all men.

What we learn from these explicit utterances of the Saviour, we infer from all His teaching and His bearing toward men. He treats them all as children of the one Father, lost, indeed, exiled from home, wanderers in a strange and alien life, degrading the powers which belong to the Lord into the service of the basest ends, but even as children whom the Father loves because He is their Father, whom He seeks because He loves, whom He will find because He seeks. There are no finer examples of the spirit which pervades God's moral economy and is the motive of His dealings with His evil off-spring than the parables of the Lost Sheep and of the Lost Piece of Silver. And the thought which fills both of them is of an ownership, a right and title in the thing lost, which that loss does not affect, and which sends the owner searching till he finds what he seeks; and grouped as they are with the parable of the Prodigal Son, their meaning is clear as day, — the truth that

God seeks men to save them because He is
theirs and they are His; He their Father, they
His children; dear to Him in spite of their evil,
precious in His sight in spite of their ruin; His
by right, though temporarily given over to the
Devil; sons still, though exiles; true sheep of
the fold, though straying and forlorn; stamped
with the image of heaven, though trampled
under foot in the rubbish and refuse of life.

IV. — THE APOSTOLIC DOCTRINE.

The apostles of Jesus Christ were not slow to
grasp their Master's meaning, and to thrust it to
the front in dealing with the world they now
went forth to convert. In various ways, according to the conditions of those to whom they
spoke, they enforced the truth that Jesus Christ
had revealed to man, — the fact of God's fatherhood, His love, and His compassion for man.
And whenever this thought is pressed upon
human attention it is always urged home with
the special appeal that men shall deport themselves as sons, and not as strangers to their
God. The truth was impressed upon Peter's
mind in the vision of the sheet let down from

heaven, in which he was taught that a Gentile in God's sight was of equal value with a Jew, — a soul to be saved, a child to be reclaimed. Paul preached it to the Athenians, when he reminded them that " we are the offspring of God." The offspring resembles the parent. And Paul's argument with the Greeks turns upon the fact that since the offspring is the image of the parent, the son is the likeness of the father, we being in the likeness of God; because His children ought not to think of Him as like lifeless, unintelligent " gold, silver, or stone." Paul uses the same thought again to enforce a practical measure upon the Christian church when he insists upon the men's praying with their heads uncovered, because man is in the image of God, — an argument which would be absolutely without point unless Paul meant to say that the image still remained in the men of Corinth.

In the epistles especially do we read the mind of Paul upon this point in unmistakable clearness. To him there is but one thought of God, and that is as a Father, humanity as one family, redemption a universal work, salvation the common destiny of the race. And whether he is bidding the Gentile rejoice in his membership in

the spiritual family or urging the Jew to make
good his descent from Abraham by an inward
sonship to God, or calling on his Christian
charges to be glad in their new knowledge of
this glorious relationship which at once ennobles
them and magnifies God's name, Paul is always
conscious of the new truth which has been revealed in Christ and is meant for every creature:
" To us there is but one God, the Father."
That name to him is the only sufficient name by
which to designate God; and that is the name
revealed through Jesus Christ. And he is em-
phatic in insisting[1] that the Christian should
think of this trait as the peculiar characteristic
of God, as He was revealed in Jesus.

In the epistle to the Ephesians[2] Paul makes
use of the same phrase, which shows that it is
to him a familiar thought, when in stating
the characteristics of Christian faith he states as
one of its articles: " One God and Father of
all, who is above all, and through all, and in
you all." Undoubtedly this is an utterance to
Christians, and therefore to those who had come
to a knowledge and a recognition of their sonship and were trying to make their lives con-

---

[1] 1 Corinthians viii. 6.   [2] Ephesians iv. 6.

form to their lineage. But just as undoubtedly
it is the statement of a truth which, though
made known to and understood only by the
Christian consciousness of that day, is a universal fact, true of and for all men. Spoken to
those who have entered into the enjoyment of
their sonship with all its hallowed privileges, it
is yet a truth which applies to those who are yet
ignorant of its inclusiveness, and careless of its
import. Dr. Ellicott, Bishop of Gloucester and
Bristol, has a most excellent and pertinent
thought upon this passage: " God is said to be
the 'Father of all.' We cannot limit this im-
mense fatherhood; although undoubtedly the
context shows that the immediate reference is
to those who are His children by adoption in
Jesus Christ. The Church is essentially catholic,
inheriting by special gift what is the birthright
of all humanity; incapable of perfection till all
be drawn into that closer sonship, yet having
neither the right nor the desire to deny that
outside His pale at any moment the wider fatherhood of God extends." [1]

But we may not neglect another view of our
theme, which engaged the attention of the sacred
writers.

[1] Handy Commentary.

A large part of what they have to say concerns itself with those who disobey the Divine law, and separate themselves from the Father's love and presence. For these there are strong and searching words, stern, uncompromising, bitter. They are called "aliens" and "strangers" and "foreigners." They are pronounced "enemies." They are dismissed as "bastards and not sons." They are described as "children of the Devil," doing the works of their father, the Devil. And the question is asked, How are we to reconcile these terrible phrases with the teaching that all men are God's children? Are these to be called the children of God, with an inalienable title to the kingdom of heaven? Is Judas as truly a child of God as John? Has Nero as inalienable a claim on God's love as Paul? Is the fatherhood of God extended to these degraded, depraved, rebellious, and utterly vicious creatures as fall under the denunciations of all righteous and conscientious men? What shall be said to these searching questions?

In the first place, it is to be remarked that such phrases as these refer not to the native and essential nature of the soul, and its relation back to its source, but to an acquired character, the outcome of evil choice and vicious living. There is no dispute over the fact of sin, nor over the ruinous consequences of sin, nor over the estrangement that sin creates between man and God, nor about the injury done to the image of God imprinted on man's nature. These are facts of human experience. And there are no words too vigorous and scathing to describe the moral state of the reprobate and sinful soul. Sin does make man an alien, a stranger, and a foreigner toward God. It cuts him off from the enjoyment of his birthright. It interrupts his blessings, and delays his inheritance of the joys of the kingdom of heaven. But it does not, for it cannot, alter man's innate and constitutional relation to God.

The creation of man in the image of God means, if it means anything, that man is constitutionally in the likeness of his Maker. He has in him all the capacities of a true son of God, — capacities which sin may pervert, corrupt, deprave, deaden, but not destroy, not annihilate. And those capacities, even while they are unfulfilled, are the inalienable claim of the soul to the position of sonship. Is not your babe your child? Must he grow to maturity, and learn to obey and love you, before he is your son; or do his very capacities, his constitution, his germinal characteristics, entitle him to your love, your care, your oversight as a father? Does a man disown his offspring and refuse to acknowledge them as children until they have come to reflect the parental virtues? Are they deprived of the privilege of calling him their father until they are old enough and disciplined enough to give a free obedience? Capacity for sonship *is* sonship, when it inheres in the very constitution of the offspring. And whatever inheres in that constitution cannot be lost out of it, except by the annihilation of life itself.

Moreover, if we were to accept the assertion that God is not the Father of those who have not yet come to love Him, we involve ourselves in a most serious difficulty. God creates every new soul that is born into this life. It is a fresh creation from the Divine Hand, and it brings with it a new breath from God's creative spirit. The old answer to the question, "Who made you?" is still the first upon our lips. "It is He that hath made us, and not we ourselves." But if God makes every one of us, He either makes us in His image or not in His image. If He makes us in His image, then He makes us by very birth and constitution His children. If He does not make us in His image, but creates us in total corruption and evil, turning naturally and inevitably to sin, how can He hold us guilty for conforming to the very constitution He has given us? You cannot blame a dog for biting. You cannot blame a child of the Devil, born so, constituted so, essentially and radically and totally inclined to the works of the Devil, for turning to devilish things.

But evidently when Jesus says to the Jews whom He would rebuke, "Ye are of your father the Devil," He uses the phrase only in that figurative way in which they call themselves "children of Abraham." They were exhibiting a malignant and devilish spirit, and in so far were properly styled the children of the Devil. They had not recognized their true kinship to God by a godly behavior; and so they were denying their true relation and assuming a kinship of disposition and character to Satan himself.

V. — The Doctrine of Adoption.

But there is still more to be said, before we have fairly stated the New Testament doctrine of the fatherhood. There is no doubt a special sense in which this relation applies to the obedient child, which is not and cannot be true of the disobedient. It is a common habit of men to say of one who repeats in himself the character and peculiar personal traits of his father, " You are your father's own child." The meaning is clear enough. Moral likeness is a realization of what the natural relationship stands for; and so the moral likeness of man to his Father carries into effect all the blessed consequences of his sonship, which are conditioned upon his obedience and love for their full bestowment. God is the Father of all souls. But He is especially the Father of those who by the birth from above have come into the practice and spirit of the divine life. A man is always God's child in the sense that he is made in God's image, is created by God's love, is sustained by His care, is the object of His affectionate providence in training and education. But he is never a true son, a good son, never anything but a prodigal, a wayward, unfaithful, false, and degenerate son, until he has sought to return his Father's love, and render to Him a filial obedience. And so while God is the Father of all souls, He stands in a peculiarly near and tender relationship to those who acknowledge their sonship and perform their filial duties. He holds this attitude too by virtue of the same fact which makes Him, as Paul calls Him, " The Saviour of all men, specially of those that believe." [1]

Until Christ opened the minds of men to the transcendent fact, the fatherhood of God was an unknown truth. They lived in ignorance of it, or with the most shadowy knowledge of it. But when He who bore in Himself at once the divine and the human nature unfolded to man His real standing in God's sight and the real tie by which God's heart was bound to Him, He brought a new motive to bear upon human life, and revealed a new power in connection with it. For by the knowledge He gave them, Jesus Christ made men understand whose children they were; and by the spirit He imparted to them He helped them to become in reality what they nominally already were, that is, the sons of God. The child is the man in the intent of his Creator; but he has yet to become a man in stature and in faculties. In a sense, and in a very true and

[1] 1 Timothy iv. 10.

literal sense, too, he has yet to become what he already is. And so when we come to the development of the spiritual life, a man may be a son of God, and yet reject his own right and disown his own sonship. And it is only where he has accepted his rights and acted in harmony with his own nature that he becomes in the fullest sense a son. That is the meaning of John when he writes : " He came unto His own, and His own received Him not. But to as many as received Him, to them gave He power to become the sons of God." Christ came to His own countrymen, kinsmen, brethren in the commonwealth of Israel. They received Him not. But others did, here and there one, a growing number, Jew and Gentile indiscriminately, "and to as many as received Him, to them gave He power to become the sons of God," in the full sense of a consciousness of relation and a new life based upon it. This is the new birth, the birth from above, namely, the sense of sonship received into the soul, and the desire to live according to its requirements. It is the discovery of God's relation to us, and the desire to realize that relationship on our own part. It is the birth within us of the dispositions which flow naturally from a knowledge of our sonship and a sense of its duties, its privileges, its joys. And it is this· experience which raises us from a merely nominal and latent sonship, a sonship inherent but undeveloped, existing but unrealized, into a sonship which is actual, recognized, and appropriated by the soul.

It follows that no man can become a son of God in this secondary and special sense until he has been renewed in affections and in will. As long as he persists in evil he is cast out from the presence of the Father; he takes the place of an alien and a stranger. And he never can enter into the possession of his birthright until by a change of heart, a disposition born from above, he seeks the things which God loves and turns from those which God abhors.

Now this change involves a change in the soul's relations to God, and of God to the soul; *but it establishes no new relationship.* God was man's Father before, as He is now; only He was the Father of a rebellious and defiant child, who had given himself over to the doing of all unfilial things. And He is a Father still, and no more than that, to the obedient and loving child who does His will and loves His law. There is a *change of relations, but no change in relationship.*

The language of the parable of the Prodigal Son is decisive upon this point. The Saviour makes the father in that touching story refer to the wayward one, even in his sins, as still his child. " For this my son was dead, and is alive again ; he was lost, and is found." He was a lost son, he was a dead son, but always he was a son ; and his return, his restoration, only change his relations to his father and his father's relations to him, without in the least affecting the relationship which was in its very nature unchangeable. Even so the sinful soul does not by its sins destroy its relationship to God nor God's relationship to it. It only brings about a change of relations within that unchangeable relationship. This derangement of right relations between God and His sinning child must continue as long as the sin, and no longer. But in the reconciliation of man to his father which comes with repentance and regeneration, he enters into a higher and better relation with God, which has received, in the apostolic writings, the name of " adoption."

Now in this term, for whose use we are indebted to the apostles, we touch a new phase of man's life with God. The apostle John, besides the words already quoted, addresses his brethren in Christ in these words: "Behold what manner of love the Father hath bestowed upon us, that we should be called the sons of God." Paul declares that they who " are led by the spirit of God, they are the sons of God;"[1] that they have received "the spirit of adoption" which gives them the right to say, " Abba, Father;"[2] that if they are children, " then [are they] heirs;"[3] that if they become pure God "will be a father" unto them;[4] and he assures the saints at Ephesus that " God hath predestinated us to the adoption of children."[5]

In these and like passages we find the teaching that there is a phase of sonship, an exercise of the Divine fatherhood, which belongs especially to the obedient and the loyal, — those who have given themselves to God; those who have returned from their wanderings in transgression and sin. This reinstatement of the sinner in the favor of his Father, this restoration of the blessings from which sin always cuts him off, is called " adoption." It involves more than a mere restoration to innocence. Salvation is a larger

---

[1] Romans viii. 14. [2] Ibid. 15. [3] Ibid. 17.
[4] 2 Corinthians vi. 17, 18. [5] Ephesians i. 5, 6.

word than mere restoration of an old status. It includes the removal of the corruptions and depravities of sin, and adds to it the induction of the soul into a higher spiritual standing, won in the long, hard struggle with sin, — the bestowment of a new disposition, not in the likeness of Adam, but of the Christ. We may not dwell on this thought. We leave it with a citation from Dr. T. J. Crawford's admirable treatise of " The Fatherhood of God." He says : " In the carrying out of this process of restitution, there are high and potent agencies employed, with which we can scarcely suppose humanity to be brought into contact without having all its original elements not only restored but gloriously elevated and transfigured, insomuch that *far more than was lost in Adam shall be gained in Christ.*" [1]

VI. — THE TEACHING OF THE FATHERS.

It would utterly transcend the limits of a single thesis to develop and illustrate this doctrine of the Scriptures more fully. Enough has been done in tracing the development of the

[1] The Fatherhood of God, p. 141.

thought from its early presentation to Israel down to its joyful acceptance by the apostles of our Lord, to show that it is unquestionably the great and transcendent fact of revelation, the radical idea of the gospel, the fruitful stem from which successively spring forth the branching doctrines of the Christian faith. We must pass on to review in the briefest way the development of the doctrine in the minds of the later learners at the feet of the Christ, whose thought has helped to develop the truths of Christianity into their more formal statements. In the obscure period of the apostolic fathers, we have but scant means of tracing the progress of this doctrine. But we know that Saint Clement of Rome exhorted his disciples to look steadfastly " unto the Father and Maker of the whole world." The " Epistle to Diognetus " foreshadows the spirit of the age so soon to follow. The writer lays especial stress upon the fact that man may imitate God, because God has made him in His own image. " For God has loved mankind," he says, " on whose account He made the world, to whom He rendered subject all the things that are in it, to whom He gave reason and understanding, to whom alone He imparted the privilege of

3.

looking upward to Himself, whom He formed
after His own image, to whom He has sent
His only begotten Son." [1]

Clement, the eminent head of the catechetical
school at Alexandria, held, in the words of
Professor Allen, that in the redemption there is
" no readjustment or restoration of a broken
relationship between God and humanity, but
rather the revelation of a relationship which had
always existed, indestructible in its nature, ob-
scured but not obliterated by human ignorance
and sin." [2]

Dr. Bigg, in the Bampton Lectures for 1886,
also says of Clement: " He looks upon redemption, not as the restitution of that which was
lost at the fall, but as the crown and consum-
mation of the destiny of man, leading to a
righteousness such as Adam never knew, and to
heights of glory and power as yet unscaled and
undreamed. 'The Word of God became Man,
in order that thou also mayest learn from Man
how man becomes God.' "

Origen made no distinction between the natural state of Adam and that in which all mankind

[1] Epistle to Diognetus, ch. x.
[2] Continuity of Christian Thought, p. 57.

have since been born. Athanasius taught that in
order to know God He must be looked for in the
soul. The soul sees the image of God in itself,
and in itself conceives the Father.[1] And he
who formulated the faith the Church has always
held in the incarnation, declared of God that
His essential nature was love, and that the inner-
most being of Deity was to be known in its last
analysis as the Father. We cannot better state
the theology which prevailed until the unhappy
day when the genius of Augustine in the interests and the name of Christianity perverted its
creed and poisoned its spirit, than by citing the
words in which Professor Allen describes it in
the Bohlen Lectures for 1883: " It followed
as a necessary sequence from the first principle
of Greek theology, — the doctrine of the Divine immanence, — that man should be viewed
as having a constitutional kinship with Deity.
By the image of God in man was understood
an inalienable heritage, a spiritual or ethical
birthright, which could not be forfeited. Deity
and humanity were not alien one to the other ;
and it was their constitutional relationship
which made the incarnation not only possible,

[1] Contra Gentes, c. 34.

but a necessary factor in the process of redemption." [1]

But with the advent of the great theologian on whose thought has been modelled the creed of all the Western branch of the Christian Church, there came a new spirit into the Church. The doctrine of original sin, imputed sin, total depravity, dates clearly from the mind of Augustine. According to its terms, humanity is absolutely separated from God in the sin of Adam. The guilt of sin involves the whole family of man. The effect of that sin was to destroy utterly in man the image of God in which man was created. Adam lost for himself and his descendants the relationship in which he was begotten; and through the corrupt and utterly depraved natures they inherit from their ancestor, human souls are cut off from God; and everything akin to the divine in reason, in conscience, in will, is utterly destroyed. They are children of God no longer, they are only His creatures. And it is only by the absolute will of God, electing whom He will, rejecting whom He chooses, that souls are received again into that union with God which

[1] Bohlen Lectures, p. 177.

was forfeited by the first man, and denied to all his posterity.

Such was Augustinianism. And such is the subtle and misleading falsehood with which the soul of Christendom has wrestled from that day to this. It was perpetuated in the theology of the Church of Rome, and spun out in the metaphysics of the Schoolmen. It glowered in the awful blasphemies of Calvinism, and the revolt of Wesley and Whitefield was not strong enough to break its malign spell. And not until the intellectual and religious life of the nineteenth century, stirring in the thought of Germany and England and America, reverted to the earlier type of Christianity as interpreted by the great fathers, was the bondage of Christendom to the Bishop of Hippo broken, and the larger measure of the gospel doctrine of the Divine fatherhood comprehended anew.

The significance of the theological movement of the present age is scarcely understood as yet, even by those most active in promoting it. But it begins to be clear that it is a return to the faith of the first three centuries in the Church's history. The orthodoxy of Augustine cannot live in the air of this century. Its errors and exaggerations are destined to die out before the thoughts that fill men's souls to-day. The orthodoxy of Clement and of Origen, coming as it does into the closest relations of sympathy and support with the truths which science has most firmly established, is renewing its hold after centuries of condemnation. And in no respect is this generation more thoroughly in accord with it than in its assertion of the Divine fatherhood, and the persistence of God's image in the human soul, under all the ruin and demoralization of sin.

VII. — Divine Fatherhood and Divine Love.

It is impossible for the student of this truth as it has been revealed to humanity by Jesus Christ to escape one or two leading and impressive facts, which are necessary inferences from this attitude of God to man. We have presented the scriptural testimony to the truth entirely from one side, because the denial of the universality of the fatherhood is based upon the change which has taken place in human nature since the fall. The entire weight of the imposing structure of text and argument in refutation of

God's universal fatherhood rests upon the assumption that the Divine image in man has been utterly lost, and that this loss annihilates the relationship. But is that true? Is there not another side from which we are bound to approach this relationship in order to discover its full significance? Fatherhood has two sides. It depends as much upon the nature of God as it does upon the nature of man. It rests not alone upon the perpetuity of the Divine image in man, but also upon the Divine nature in whose image man was created. God is man's father, by virtue of what He is in His own infinite nature. The creation of man was the spontaneous act of the Divine will. God made man in His image, of His own choice and by His own volition, and in creating him assumed a relationship toward him. Now that relationship no act of man can annul. That is true of the earthly manifestation of this divine relationship. He who begets a child is always and forever that child's father; and there are obligations, as there are sentiments, growing out of that fact, which no act of the child can destroy or alter or modify. Once a father, man is always a father. For though he seek to evade his duties, or with-

hold his love, he cannot abolish the unalterable
fact that he is a father, and that his own act has
sealed upon him certain unchangeable obligations.   More than that; if he be a true father
there is nothing which can make him change his
relationship to his child.   He finds it ingrained
in his very nature.   He must be a father to
that child, no matter how the child deports himself in return.   The child may lose all semblance
of likeness to his father; he may become absolutely imbecile, and be bereft of reason, intelligence, and every mental likeness to his parent.
Still, his father will not be the less his father,
nor less under bond to care for and protect his
unhappy child.   That child may fall into the
lowest degradation, may lose all moral likeness
to his kindred, may sear his conscience and
blunt every spiritual perception.   Still, that does
not shift the relationship, does not alter the obligations of fatherhood.   These persist, unalterable by any act of the child; and the nobler the
mould in which that parental nature is cast, and
the more Christ-like it is, the more impossible
does it become for it to change its attitude and
be anything but the friend, the guardian, the
lover of its offspring.

That this is the central principle of the Divine fatherhood; that it rests on the spontaneous disposition of God toward His children, and not on any variable or fluctuating condition of the soul of man; that God fathers man's spirit because of what He is in His own infinite nature, — we find corroboration in the Christian doctrine of the atonement. That dogma describes work which God has done for man, not by virtue of anything man has done or failed to do, but by reason of the love for man which wells up out of God's own inexhaustible being. God sends His Son to save the world, not for anything man has done, but because He loves man, and desires to rescue him from the bondage of sin. "God was in Christ reconciling the world unto Himself." [1] "But God commendeth His love toward us in that while we were yet sinners Christ died for us." [2] "In this was manifested the love of God toward us, because that God sent His only begotten Son into the world, that we might live through Him. Herein is love, not that we loved God, but that He loved us, and sent His Son to be the propitiation for our sins." [3]

[1] 2 Corinthians v. 19.   [2] Romans v. 8.
[3] 1 John iv. 9, 10.

The ground of the atonement is the love, unchanging and unchangeable, which God entertains toward those whom He has created in His own image. The impulse to save and redeem the souls of men comes from the spontaneous and irresistible love and grace of God the Father. Upon that fact, finally, God's fatherhood rests; and nothing can change it except the annihilation of His children, so that there is nothing for God to be a father to; or the utter transformation of His own nature.

This, after all has been said, is the real bond of unity which makes a single family of the human race. This is the great spiritual fact, the inner truth which stands in such close relations to the outward signs of kinship which mark our race. The anatomist takes man's frame to pieces, and finds in its very structure something which sets him off in a different group from every other form of organic life. The antiquarian hunts out his remains, his early arts and simple skill, and traces common needs and common modes of meeting them. The historian recognizes common aims running through all his attempts at building states and establishing his social life. Philanthropy points to his suffering, counts his sighs, and notes the tears which flow alike from all human eyes, and bids us mark that men share a common lot of blessing or of bane. But these, after all, are resemblances which serve to group men by their outward peculiarities. They form a sort of artificial system, so long as we rest in them and go no deeper. But the gospel, announcing the fact of man's sonship to God, accounts for these likenesses, as well as discovers the real source of the unity of the race. In that thrilling fact we have a reason why one man is like another. It is for the same reason that all the children in one family have blue eyes, or light hair, or a fair complexion. The mark of their parentage is stamped upon them. That fundamental fact accounts for all the others. And this grand fundamental truth that all men are God's children explains all man's various struggles, his yearning heart, his creative mind, his aspiring instincts, his unfolding affections. It is the God-nature working to full maturity. Children are not related because they look alike; they look alike because they are related. Human beings, too, are not called brethren because they have so much in common. They possess these common traits because they are brethren, children of one Father. The "touch of nature" which "makes the whole world kin" is the likeness of man to his Maker. And it is an unspeakable privilege to us all, who are so often classified according to our weaknesses and our sins, and reminded of our likeness to each other on the ground of our universal sinfulness and sorrow, to come up to the summit of this truth, which lifts us so high and gives us so noble a dignity. Thank God, the real reason why we are alike is not because we are so easily tempted, not because we love evil, not because we are ignorant, weak, or wicked, but because we are the children of the Most High; because one God hath created us.

The line of kinship, then, includes all human souls. It makes no boundary between races or nations. It classes the savage in his imperfection with a Plato or a Wilberforce. For the savage has a soul — nay, is a soul — as truly as the sage or the reformer. He bears God's likeness; he is sustained by God's life; he is the recipient of His love. The powers of heaven and earth, visible and invisible, are enlisted for him as truly as they are for the saints or the seraphim.

God looks with impartial tenderness on the dweller by the tropic Amazon, and the denizen of smoky London. The sun that girdles the earth every day looks on no face of all the human kind which does not share the common birth-mark. The sailor on the reeling deck, and he who for his sake watches the light upon the solitary reef; the artisan at his toil, the soldier pouring out his blood in battle, and the little babe upon its mother's breast; the judge upon the bench, and the unhappy convicts in scores of dreary prisons; prince and peasant; statesman and serf; the godly and the sinful; the youth and the grandsire,—these all being the offspring of one Creator are His souls, His sons and daughters. No matter whether a man dwells in high places or low, whether he keeps the law of God or breaks it, still he is God's child always and forever. Manhood itself is the divine quality,—the trait which links us to our God.

It follows from these premises that whatever conclusions as to the destiny of souls are drawn from the nature of God and His dispositions toward men, cannot be undermined by any assault upon the relationship which is assumed in calling God the father of all souls, because those

conclusions rest upon no mere playing with
words and logical or theological niceties over
terms. The faith in the final triumph of God
does not depend upon the name we may give to
God, but upon the love which He bears to souls, —
a love which makes the name of "father" more
expressive of His real attitude to men than any
other known to them. If men choose to quibble
over the doctrine of the fatherhood of God, and
cling to the doctrine of total depravity, and in-
sist that a corrupt soul is not a child of God,
they are welcome to do so. They do not touch
the great central dogma of Christian faith, on
which Universalism plants itself and defies dis-
lodgement. That truth is: That God loves men,
all men, sinful men, depraved men; loves them
so much that He sent His Son to save them;
loves them without return and without recognition; loves them' with a love which could only
find its adequate expression in the cross on Cal-
vary; loves them with a love which is without
variableness or shadow of turning. His love is
unaffected by the sin of man, which only rouses
it to sacrifice for the sinner's sake. And His
love does not rest upon the maintenance of a
fixed and definite likeness of an image to its

original. It grows out of the self-sustained nature of the everlasting God, which nature is, in its last essence, a nature of love. In other words, and briefly, the love of God does not grow out of the fatherhood of God, but the fatherhood of God has its root in the love of God. And since the New Testament expressly declares the love of God for the sinful soul, is it a great stretch of interpretation to infer the fatherhood of God from the same declarations? At all events it makes but little difference whether we rest our faith in the blessed destiny on the fatherhood of God or the love of God. Both describe the attitude and relation of God to man, out of which it is safe to infer that good must come at last to all.

This is the great truth to which the mission of Jesus upon earth bears conspicuous witness. His whole life was an embodiment of God's disposition toward men, and His death set forth yet more gloriously the sacred fact of God's paternal love. In life and in death Jesus was testifying to the fatherhood of God, and to the affectionate care which that relationship implies. And the peculiar and salient feature of the Divine love which Jesus manifested to man was its free and unconstrained quality. Everything about Christ's life for man, every sacrifice and every duty, was a voluntary gift to humanity. His will was under no duress. He was acting freely. He made a free offering of Himself to the cause of human salvation, — the reconciliation of the child to his Father, the restoration of harmony between earth and heaven. But in our Saviour we are taught to see our God; in what He did for us, what God is ever doing for us; in the attitude of His spirit toward us, a sign and proof of God's eternal bearing toward His offspring. As Christ's love for the world depended on nothing that the world had done for Him, so the Father's love of His children depends not on their nature or works, but upon His own. He loves them spontaneously, because it is His nature to love them. So that however man may be disposed toward God, the Father never changes His disposition toward man. Even in his sins and wanderings God is loving him, though varying the mode of manifesting that love to suit the needs of the soul. Jesus dying for a world which had rejected and crucified Him, Jesus praying in His last moments for the very men whose sins hung Him on the cross, is an everlasting type of the Father whose love is equally bestowed on all mankind.

This is the very essence of New Testament teaching. The apostle Paul declares that "God was in Christ, reconciling the world unto Himself," [1] — a plain announcement that God takes the initiative in this holy work. He says again, "God commendeth (or proveth) His love toward us, in that, while we were yet sinners, Christ died for us." [2] John says: "In this was manifested the love of God toward us, because that God sent His only begotten Son into the world, that we might live through Him. Herein is love, not that we loved God, but that He loved us, and sent His Son to be the propitiation for our sins." [3] Jesus Himself accounts for His own presence in this world in the words, " For God so loved the world." [4] The very essence of God's love is its spontaneousness, which lifts it above all possible conditions, all limitation by man's sinfulness, and makes it dependent only on the nature of the Father.

The parables of Jesus always enforce the same truth. They are full of this doctrine of a

[1] 2 Corinthians v. 19.　　[2] Romans v. 8.
[3] 1 John iv. 10.　　[4] John iii. 16.

love in God's heart which antedates and transcends any goodness and any merit on man's part, and is self-originating and self-subsistent. That wonderful series of parables which seems to speak the very heart of the Master, and illustrates the inner spirit of the gospel, — the stories of the Lost Sheep, the Lost Piece of Silver, and the Prodigal Son, — these are all so many illustrations of the boundless and spontaneous nature of Divine love, a love which does not need to be won by service, nor bought with the price of love returned, since it is continually anticipating our affection and our duty, and far outrunning the swiftness of our gratitude. The shepherd is following the sheep in his wanderings. The woman is searching for the lost money. The father is loving the prodigal so dearly that he watches for him and sees him yet a great way off and runs to meet him. In every case there is the implication that God's love is original and spontaneous, lying behind all the agencies and the measures by which man's salvation is wrought. Nor can the inference be avoided, that as long as the nature of God endures, this love will urge Him to labors for man's good, — labors which can no more be limited to the brief years of this life than the power of gravitation can be confined to our planet.

VIII. — Fatherhood and Human Depravity.

But we are not willing to rest the matter here, for if we did it might seem that we conceded by faint implication the doctrine that human nature has lost all semblance of the Divine nature, and that in it the image of God is totally destroyed. That we are far from doing. This is the dark, discredited doctrine of total depravity, disguised, softened, asserted indirectly, but at bottom the ancient discreditable falsehood as to human nature which has weighed down the theology of fourteen centuries. No clear-sighted student of theology will for a moment deny the corruption, nay, the depravity of human nature, nor the stern law which entails the curse by heredity. All that is conceded. But to say that this depravity can totally wreck God's image in the soul, that it obliterates the very semblance of the Divine in the nature of man, that it wholly defiles him "in all faculties and parts of soul and body," is utterly inconsistent with the Scripture we have cited, and is foreign to the whole

tenor of theological teaching up to the time of
Augustine. When we speak of the image of God
in which man was created we must admit, as
Dr. Mark Hopkins truly says, that "the image
of God to be thus created was not anything incidental or that could be separated from man,
but must consist in something so essential to
him that if he should lose it he would cease to
be a man. . . . So long as man continues to be
rational, moral, and free, and hence capable of
knowing God, he will be in His image; and
when he ceases to be rational, moral, and free he
will no longer be man." [1]   Or in the fine phrase
of Canon Liddon: "The fall of man consists
rather in the privation of God's supernatural
grace than in a positive corruption of all his
faculties, such as has been imagined by some
modern divines; and as the doctrine was understood by the ancient Church, the fall left human
nature dismantled indeed, but something less
than a shapeless ruin. . . . In each of Adam's
children the Divine image was still traceable in
its twofold features of intelligence and freedom,
though the one was darkened, and the other

---

[1] Scriptural Idea of Man, p. 26.

impaired." [1]   That is the statement of one of the most eminent and profound of English theologians; and it may well serve as a summary of the doctrine of this thesis.   Even so gloomy and pessimistic a Methodist as Dr. L. T. Townsend concedes " the fact of the existence of an inhering or adhering goodness in human nature, which may be termed germinal in the sense of possessing undeveloped elements." [2]

Let us note one other important corollary of the truth we are discussing.   If it were true that there is no trace left in sinful men of the Divine image, there could be no ground of appeal to man to bring him to repentance.   There is no use in calling a physician to restore health in an organism that is absolutely destroyed.   So if the mind has parted with reason, there is no ground on which to stand in appealing to the darkened intellect.   If, then, there were nothing in man which allied him to God, no common life by virtue of his descent from Deity, then there is no power conceivable which could make man understand the call God makes upon him to repent, amend his ways, and take his place as a

[1] University Sermons, first series, p. 304.
[2] Lost Forever, p. 183.

child in God's blessed company of the redeemed. The nature of man, with its latent spiritual powers, the undeveloped image of the Father, is the basis of God's work in developing him into the divine life. If it were not for that germinal nature which answers to the appeal of its Creator, man could never exert the slightest effort of will toward his own salvation; and if it were true that the Divine image is utterly destroyed by sin, then He who came to save sinners might as well have been sent to a race of graven images or a family of pine-trees. "The human heart," says Newman Smyth, "with all its passions and impurities, is still the truest mirror in which we can behold the invisible God." And it is this God-likeness in our hearts which makes them answer at all to the persuasions of the Holy Spirit. If the germ and elements of eternal life had not been folded within our hearts in our natural birth, they would never be unfolded in the new birth, — the birth from above. When man turns away from sin and seeks the face of God, his own nature is answering that Nature in whose image he was formed, and the soul is rising into its own true life.

Universalism, like all kindred phases of the

new theology, puts the doctrine of regeneration on a firmer basis in reason and in Scripture than it ever had on the artificial foundations reared by Augustinianism. For it is asserted as a process involving known laws and analogies, just as Christ delivered it to man, and not as a device of spiritual magic, or extraordinary and irregular exercise of Divine force. It is asserted as a necessary step in man's induction into the higher life, as a necessity of the soul. Man cannot rise upward into the life of the spiritual world until he has been born of the Spirit, any more than he can enter the natural world till he has been born of the flesh. But the second birth is as much a universal necessity as the first, and, like the birth in the body, is, in the words of Dr. Munger, "a constructive, not a reconstructive process." It is the step which every sinner will at last be constrained to take, not by the arbitrary will of Deity, but by the necessities of his own nature, — the law of that constitution in which he was formed, when God proposed to gather together in one "all things in Christ." For this great fact and law of spiritual life, Universalism has borne no uncertain testimony. The necessity of regeneration has never been denied; and

least of all is its denial involved in the universal
fatherhood, which is the very corner-stone on
which it rests. Universalism simply asserts for
all men, as a law of the life of the soul, what the
traditional Christianity limits to the few and the
favored.

It is the strength of the new theology that it
places this great fact of the spiritual life upon
an impregnable basis. It treats regeneration as
a normal and natural fact of man's experience,
as much in the nature of things as the change
of the embryo into the child, and of the child
into the man. Nay, more; we may use the
terms of science, and assert that Christianity
declares what we call regeneration to be the
evolution of a higher humanity out of a lower.

There is another form which is sometimes used
as an alternative reading of the passage in which
Jesus describes the new birth, which renders
it, " Except a man be born *from above,* he cannot see the kingdom of God."[1] That explains
the place of this great experience in the cate-
gories of science. Every advance of species
from a lower to a higher grade, or every creation of a higher to supersede a lower, is an in-

[1] John iii. 3.

flowing of life from above,—of *the* Life from above which creates us all.

In the exercise of His fatherly love and the unfolding of His paternal providence toward man, God brings him at last to this crowning step in the long ascent of evolution. It will be the highest in all probability that we shall ever see taken in this world. It will be the process by which this earth shall receive a new race, as far above the man of the present age as he is above the cave-dweller and the bushman. This is the goal of God's fatherly purpose for man; and this goal is to be attained through the spiritual renewal and uplifting of man which is called the birth from above.

IX. — FATHERHOOD AND THE PROBLEM OF EVIL.

No survey of the doctrine of the fatherhood of God, even the most cursory, can leave untouched its relations to the existence of evil. The presence of this element in the creation is a fact always hard to reconcile with the goodness of the Divine nature. This was the problem which tried the faithful heart of Job, and is the refrain

which runs through that sublime epic of suffering, which has anticipated all that Hartmann
or Schopenhauer or Mill or Ingersoll ever al-
leged against the doctrine of the Divine love
and fatherhood. This is the problem which
presented itself to the mind of Paul when he
made that immortal answer, — the only possible
solution and the only needful one: " For the
creature was made subject to vanity, not will-
ingly, but by reason of him who hath subjected
the same in hope." [1] For whatever may be said
of any other theories concerning evil and the
Divine love, it is certain that there is one which
offers a reasonable and consistent interpretation
of this mystery, so far as any is possible in our
present condition of ignorance and limitation.
No man can do more than indicate a rational
theory on this matter. For the full demonstra-
tion of its truth we must await the fulfilment
of the ages. " The crucial test of a thoughtful
mind," says some one, " is a sense of the mystery of life." But there is an appreciable relief
to that sense when it approaches the facts of
evil and of sin in some such faith as the com-
mon-sense of the age is coming to have in the

---

[1] Romans viii. 20.

teachings of the gospel, — that this is a growing world, developing toward some high end whose attainment shall explain the windings of the way by which it was reached. If we can see any beneficent end to moral evil, both for the creation as a whole and for every individual in it, we can reconcile evil with the goodness of God. If we find reasons for believing that such an issue is possible for every human soul, we can believe the fact compatible with the fatherhood of God. Present evil is perfectly consistent with infinite power and love if it can be shown that it is temporary, transitional, — a phase of existence, and not a finality. The · pain, the strife, the suffering of the world's early age become less formidable in their challenge to faith, if we see in them the " growing pains " of an expanding creation. The feuds and fightings which have cursed the past seem less hard to reconcile with a benevolent purpose when we see how they have paved the way for an era when wars shall cease. The cloud of personal bereavement and grief has a silver lining when we have learned how afflictions purify and deepen the springs of life. So, too, if there is any fruitage of salvation to grow out of penalty and retribu-

tion, it is not hard to believe penalty salutary
and beneficent.   And if it appear that out of
the deep furrowings of sin there may spring up
better dispositions, and the wrath of man, under
the care and influence of God, turn to praise,
then the deeps of hell itself are not profound
enough to hide the fact of a paternal purpose,
both wise and loving, in the moral economy of
human life.   Now this solution of the dark
problem is proffered us to-day, not only by the
champions of religious faith, but also by the
very high-priest of the scientific philosophy.
" Evil," says Herbert Spencer, " perpetually tends
to disappear ; " and he adds a graphic summary
of reasons why " the things we call evil and
immorality must disappear." [1]   Mr. John Fiske,
too, in his remarkable monograph on " The
Destiny of Man," declares : " Strife and sorrow
shall disappear, peace and love shall reign su-
preme. . . . The kingdoms of this world shall
become the kingdom of Christ, and He shall
reign forever and ever." [2]   And what is this
but the teaching of the great Apostle himself,
when he declares, " The creature itself also
shall be delivered from the bondage of corrup-

[1] Social Statics, pp. 74, 78.   [2] The Destiny of Man, p. 118.

tion into the glorious liberty of the children of God " ?[1]

In this thought of the creation and all its evils, we have ample ground on which to stand in faith in the fatherhood and love of God, working from age to age for the perfecting and blessing of His creation. Once admit the thought that all the past and all the present are looking forward; building up powers and resources for the future to use and draw upon ; training and disciplining intuitions and aptitudes, senses, functions, volitions ; laying deep courses of foundation-stone on which to raise the fair structure of a better, a holier life, — and we have a ground on which to stand in hope. If it be allowed us to say and believe that the universe is not stationary but growing, its destiny one of peace and harmony, its sufferings incidental to a higher enjoyment, we can afford to suspend our gloomy judgments, give faith her rights, and frankly facing every mysterious evil, from the crushing of a fly to the overwhelming of a nation, still believe

> " That nothing walks with aimless feet,
> That not one life shall be destroyed,
> Or cast as rubbish to the void,
> When God hath made the pile complete.

[1] Romans viii. 21.

" That not a worm is cloven in vain,
    That not a moth with vain desire
    Is shrivelled in a fruitless fire,
    Or but subserves another's gain."

But here let it be said, with the utmost em-
phasis, that it is upon this theory of the Divine
government alone that the Divine goodness can
be vindicated or the Divine fatherhood main-
tained. The assumption that evil must eternally
exist, a blot upon the creation and a drawback
to its harmony; that sin is destined to prolong
itself, contrary to the will of God and the prayers
and struggles of humanity,—this thought under-
mines all the faith we are striving to maintain
in God's loving rule, and brings us face to face
with most despairing conclusions in regard to
God's ability or His desire. Eternal sin and
eternal penalty, if they be facts, are utterly un-
mitigated by any ray of light. They are a black
curse on the creation. They are a reproach to
God's love ; for they are without redeeming
features, without purpose, and without results.
They load souls with pain which does them no
good, which only exasperates and maddens,
without the least tendency either to redeem or
to destroy. And so, like any theory about

natural evil which makes it appear a perpetual
element in the creation, they are incompatible
with a benevolent scheme of things, and, by consequence, with a benevolent Creator and Ruler.

It is the privilege, then, of believers in the
gospel of Christ and the gospel of modern science to see that through all the woe and want
and weariness of creation there runs a thread of
blessing.   Nature indeed has a hand of iron
under her velvet glove.   Her face is as stern as
it is beautiful.   Her severities press upon us on
all sides, and they are unsparing, rigorous, in-
variable.   They buffet us in her piercing winds;
they beat upon us in her withering heats; they
smite us in her fierce lightnings.   Her laws are
pitiless, and her agents titanic and remorseless.
She inflicts a thousand austerities, which at first
sight seem like cruelties.   The story of evolution
is a tale of endless conflict and violence.   Progress is a terrible struggle for supremacy.   The
way of salvation, the path to sainthood itself, is
rough and thorny, rugged with sorrows and
with denials.   But that is only the background
of the pattern which the Eternal Mind is weav-
ing on the clashing looms of life; and he who
looks with true insight already sees gleaming

threads falling into shapes of beauty and of
light. The true meaning of pain is blessing.
We do not know how evil came into this world.
We know not why God could not have made us
saints without making us suffer first. We dare
not judge the Almighty and His purposes and
methods by the poor, blind reasonings of our
human minds. But this we *know*, that all pain
is not punishment; that suffering bears in its
bosom the seeds of a diviner state; that our
crosses raise us to our crowns; that the severities we endure all issue in a higher and a happier
life. The human heart is stronger than any of
the forces which hurt it. There is no adversity,
no form of suffering or of pain, over which we
may not see some souls rising in triumph, happy
in spite of life's severity. And one single in-
stance is enough to prove that pain is consistent
with happiness, and that severity is no contra-
diction of love.

X. — FATHERHOOD AND RETRIBUTION.

Turn, in attestation of this truth, to the history of human experience, in connection with
the fact of retribution. The keenest sufferings,

the most awful severities, inflicted upon human
souls are those which wickedness produces, —
are the sequences of sin.   And these, unhap-
pily, have nearly always been interpreted as the
tokens of Divine anger, — an anger which was
without mercy and without love, inflicting ven-
geance for its own sake, and gloating over suffering as aimless as it was cruel.   But is this
the only possible view of the severities with
which God visits sin ?   Is there no benevolence
in them ?   Are they necessarily the outcome of
harshness and of hate ?   Suppose they should
be the sharp thorns of the hedges God has set
up to keep us in the way of virtue.   Suppose
they should be the uneasy bed on which no
wicked soul can lie in peace.   That would be no
impossible interpretation of them ; but it would
lend to them at once a new meaning pregnant
with hope and bright with love.

If God be a true Father, He will use all the
devices of His Divine economy to prevent misery
and foster happiness.   His laws will be framed
so as to secure that happiness.   Our good will
lie in the observance of these laws.   So that to
attain our good, we must be kept from breaking
the laws which insure it to us.   This makes hap-

piness the same thing as harmony with God's will, and unhappiness discord with that will. The labor, then, of the Divine love will be to keep us in the way of righteousness. Every device which wisdom and affection can suggest will be used to secure this end. Every induce-ment will be offered to obedience; every deter-rent will be held up to disobedience. This we find to be the law of the moral universe. All the forces of resistance are concentrated upon man to restrain him from sin. Every possible inducement is offered him to walk in the way where his virtue and his happiness both lie. When a man attempts to pass the boundaries of right, he encounters some form of pain. The farther he goes, the more he suffers. Like one who tries to penetrate a thicket, and gets him-self into worse tangles with every step he goes; like a man beating out to sea against a heavy gale, who finds every wave he meets worse than the last, — is he who deserts the strait and narrow way for some cross-cut to indulgence, some ex-cursion into the seductive fields of pleasant vice. He involves himself in worse difficulties and severer pains the farther he goes. God has no pity on him while he strays; or rather, He is *so* pitiful that He will use any severity to keep him from straying. He rains misfortunes on him, follows him with disasters, multiplies the dangers which infest his path. Of all possible courses open to the human heart, God has made the virtuous course always the easiest. Observe, we do not need to say, what is not true, that righteousness is easy. But it is easier than sin. That is an unalterable law of the creation. For every difficulty and every pain in the path of the righteous, you may count a score in that hard way in which transgressors walk. If it is hard to be good, it is harder still to be bad. And any man who yields to temptation under the impression that it is easier to do that than to resist, makes as serious a mistake as he who should decide that it was easier to lie in bed and see his house burn down about him than to get up and put out the fire.

There is a favorite principle of modern science which, like all the truth of a real science, finds an application in this realm of life. The fact we are affirming is the spiritual side of a great natural law. It is a favorite doctrine of Mr. Spencer and his school, that life develops along the line of least resistance. Every combination among the forces which have given us this earth and the life there is in it, is determined by the escape of motion in the direction where there is the strongest force or the least opposition. What the religious man calls the " course of Providence," the man of science calls the operation of natural force along the line of least resistance. All the structural changes of the earth, the progress and modification of social life, the development of physical peculiarities in the individual, and even the growth of moral habits, depend upon this broad principle. No doubt this is a generalization as true in the moral world as in the physical. The direction of Divine Providence is along the line of least resistance. Indeed, we ought rather to say that the line of the least resistance is the path Divine Providence has already marked out for itself.

The law that the fittest only survive has a moral manifestation. Stated in the terms of theology, it means the triumph of good over evil. The environment which God has created for the human soul is especially calculated to preserve good and destroy evil. The severities of Heaven lie in the direction of sin, or the backward step of the soul. And as good is the only possible attribute which can harmonize with a Divine environment, we may regard the very arrangement of the creation as a pledge of its final triumph.

Here, then, we have an explanation, and in some sense a justification, of the presence of severity in retribution as an element in God's fatherhood. It is the force which resists man's moral retrogression. It is the barrier which the Heavenly Father erects on either side of the way to keep us in a straight path. If we will wander, He provides that we shall not be unwarned and unrestrained; there shall be some admonitory experience, something to startle or deter. If gentle measures fail, then there shall be sterner ones. It is far better that we should be thus buffeted by God's severities than that we should go unhindered to destruction. " Pervading all nature," says Spencer, " we may see at work a stern discipline which is a little cruel that it may be very kind." That sentence is a key to interpret the asperities of our moral experience. God wounds that He may heal. He smites that He may uplift. He will save man all the trouble and the suffering that He can. He will make our lives as happy as we will allow Him to. And whenever a human soul is blind enough

to believe its own way best, God is not slow to
disclose to it the awful blunder it has made.

And so, if not now, yet sometime, we shall
learn to bless the Power which has led us
through experiences which try and hurt us with
their severity. It would be our way to give
up the weary march of life, but God whips us
into action with a lash of stinging needs. We
would stray into the fields of illicit pleasure,
but we find them thick with thistles. We might
be too indolent to enter in at an open heaven, if
God did not send untiring angels to rouse our
sluggard wills, to spur us to the march, and to
chase our footsteps with a relentless persistence
to the heavenly goal. These powers that seem
so adverse are the sworn allies of love. Even
the iron hand of retribution is the grasp of the
Father setting itself the faster as the soul sinks
in its sins. God might have let us go astray un-
checked. He might have held off His restraints
while we went plunging down the declivities of
sin, from bad to worse, from woe to woe, down
into infinite depths of ruin. But our Father
loves us too well to lose us. When leniency
would be destruction, He is too kind to spare us.
Hence this iron grip, this unfaltering severity,

this galling stringency of restraint, are the attributes of the eternal and unalterable love of God. And under all these disguises the tender fatherhood of God works for our good, — works to restrain and to correct; works to uplift and to chasten; works to breed in us the abhorrence of evil; works to tear away the illusions of temptation; works to conduct us through the very pains of purgatory and the pangs of perdition, into the glory of the blessed life.

> " And since these biting frosts but kill
> Some tares in me which choke or spill
> That seed Thou sow'st, blest be Thy skill!

> " Blest be Thy dew and blest Thy frost,
> And happy I to be so crost,
> And cured by crosses at Thy cost."

How clearly this beneficence of suffering appears in the case of our Ignorance and its consequences. There is no case in which it is any harder to justify the severity of Providence than just here. Why, we ask ourselves, should men suffer consequences of which they were ignorant when they incurred them? Why should we be in pain for what we did not know? A man swallows a noxious herb which he did not know was a poison, and suffers a lingering sickness in consequence. Another ignores the laws of health, and after an undue strain from excessive work, falls a victim to paralysis. And we secretly think a little reproachfully of a constitution of things which is so hard upon ignorance and inadvertence. But mark the benevolence underneath this apparent harshness. Surely it were a sad fate for man if he were to live in ignorance. He never can live his best life or reap his highest enjoyments until he has overcome the drawbacks of his own lack of knowledge. Man must be forced to seek wisdom, light, and truth, or he fails of his own heaven. But the fact that ignorance is misery is the spur which drives him out of it. "If to be ignorant were as safe as to be wise," says a keen student of human nature, "no one would become wise. And all measures which tend to put ignorance on a par with wisdom inevitably check the growth of wisdom." And so these penalties attaching to blindness teach us to open our eyes. These sharp experiences of our ignorance whet all the faculties to a keener judgment. Unpitying as it looks, it is nevertheless merciful to let men suffer for their ignorance, in order that they may become wise.

Take, for example, the severity of the administration of Heaven in its dealings with Poverty. Why should it fare so hard in this world with one who is simply unthrifty, or careless, or short-sighted, or unfortunate? What do these distresses of poverty mean? It is no help to the sympathizing heart that we lay the burden of explanation on the back of some general law, and say that it is the working out of some great principle of supply and demand, or the forcing of the weakest to the wall, in order that the strongest may survive. That does not ease the problem in the least. Want and cold, starvation and disease, are just as gaunt and dreadful after this explanation as they were before. But how if the very law which bears so heavily upon the poor man contain in itself the secret of his own elevation? Remember how necessary it is for man's highest spiritual good that he should put himself beyond the condition of precarious life, of living from hand to mouth. Note how his soul-life has grown as man has been raised above the miserable and degrading poverty of the savage. Remember how this scourge of poverty, with its raging hungers and famines, its

nakedness and cold and exposure, has been
the lash which has driven our race to become
tillers and builders and weavers. Not one of
the comforts and the elegancies of our homes
would ever have existed if some poor savage
had not been driven by his sufferings from
sun and storm to build him a rude shelter,
and so lay the corner-stone of architecture.
The wealth of the world would never have existed if it had not been for the poverty of the
world. Can we not see, in the light of that
fact, that there is a certain rude kindness even
in this hard condition of poverty? Is it not
made so hard precisely in order that men may
exert themselves to get out of it? "The power
that moves the world everywhere," says some
one, " is the power of need." It is the goad
to labor. It is the spur to zeal. It drives the
sluggard afield. It rouses the careless to take
thought. It instructs the unskilful. It forces
the imprudent to mend his ways.

XI. — THE DIVINE FATHERHOOD AND HUMAN SORROW.

We find moreover in human Sorrow an illustration of the principle of God's loving father-

hood. Men often misconceive the mission of sorrow. They misread its Divine meaning. They call it punishment; they count it a retribution; they rebel against it as an injustice, trying to see in it the recompense for some fault of which they are not aware. But sorrow is not an avenger. It comes to the pure in heart as well as to the sinful. The Saviour Himself was a man of sorrows. For sorrow is God's refining fire. It is the cleanser of hearts; it is sent to mellow the spirit, to prepare it for more hallowed life, to wear away the resistance our hearts make to God's good angels. Sorrow is like the frost that breaks great bowlders and cracks them into dust for the plant to grow in. It is like the floods which rise in some rivers, inundating vast tracts, and bearing misery and ruin at first, but leaving behind their deposits of rich soil. It is like God's lightnings which scorch through the air, but burn away its mephitic vapors. The real solace of grief lies in the sublime use the Heavenly Father makes of it to enlarge our life. That is as real and true a fact as that the Titans of the material world have all been sworn to the service of God's high

ends of blessing. And that solace is the proof
that the severity of sorrow, too, is the severity
of a Father's love.

Thus we might find mercy and tenderness
under all the severities of this life. A thread
of love runs through the sternest trials. Under
all the stern appearances of nature, unseen by
the shallow and the foolish, but known to every
sincere, loving heart which suffers, there lurks
the sweetest blessing of life. Behind this
"frowning providence," these relentless laws,
these sharp distresses, our Father hides His
everlasting love. Sorrow exists but to bless.
Poverty does the bidding of love. The hard-
ships of ignorance are mercies. The strictness
of God's requirements is fully matched by the
plenitude of the mercies which they condition.
Even His retributions deal their blows in the
name of a providence which works eternally for
man's salvation. These are the glorious truths
which shine out from behind the clouds, when
we climb the peaks of faith and insight, and
overlook the widest fields of truth. From that
height we see a Father's love shining everywhere. It illumines all the broad fields of life.
It searches out the very deeps and lights them

with hope. It knows no setting. It never burns low. It is from everlasting to everlasting. It is the redeeming ray which transfigures evil, and touches life's darkest experiences with a holy comfort.

It remains for us to dwell upon one more thought in relation to this problem of evil in the creation. It is in regard to the element of time which enters into creative methods, and which renders us peculiarly liable to misjudge and mistake them. God works in long cycles, and we are still in the beginning of His mighty undertakings.

The moral creation is not finished, but progressing. Its walls are still rising. Its towers still bear the scaffolding of the toil which carries it forward. Therefore do not judge the work till it is finished. Remember how much will develop as the toil goes on. Consider the things yet remaining undone which will change the aspect of the whole. Life is not to be judged by its present phases. The present can never be properly estimated if taken by itself. All things are to be interpreted in the light of their results, their final issue, their culmination. Creation is not to be treated like a finished cathe-

dral, whose details are all done ; much less like
a crumbling ruin, whose disintegration has be-
gun.   It is to be viewed rather as one looks at
the life and interests of an expanding city, or an
undeveloped nation.   It is not done, but doing.
Its promises are as yet far greater than its ful-
filments.   It must be clothed in the light of
hope ; for time will prove the groundlessness
of misgivings and fears.   The outcome of it all
will satisfy yearning hearts ; and the labor of
every honest soul toward the grand result will
" have praise of God."

There is no truth which needs a more vigorous enforcement upon the pessimists of our day
than this general principle.   There is no answer
to their complaints and criticisms about the
creation *except* in this truth.   The great mistake
of those who seek to undermine the belief in the
Divine fatherhood is in treating this world as
if it were a finished product, its aims all fully
developed, its resources all laid bare, its development only a circular progress in which experience repeats itself, and no more.   But if anything
may be regarded as well established in fact as well
as in faith, it is the scientific doctrine that this is
a creation in process of evolution.   It is a grow-

ing crop, a web in the loom, a tale half told, a picture but just sketched in. Even those who refuse to admit that creation shows any signs of intelligence will allow that the bearing and influence of things present on one another cannot be well understood until they have worked out to their results, in some future time. And if it be conceded that there may after all be an intelligent purpose in Nature, — a plan by which all things are working, — then by so much the more must we perpetually hold judgment in suspense upon some parts of this present life.

When an artist has projected a great picture, when he has completed all his studies, conceived his plan, and decided upon his methods, he proceeds to make his preliminary sketches. He draws his various figures, in such postures and with such general expression as he means them to have in the canvas where he will finally place them. They are roughly done at first, and taken by themselves suggest no adequate notion of what the general composition will be. Perhaps he even paints each sketch with some elaboration. But even then it would be impossible to make a fair estimate of any of these carefully studied figures, or pronounce upon their coloring; be-

'cause in the mind of the artist every one of these details has a definite relation to every other, and neither face nor figure, outline nor color, can be understood except as it is thought of in connection with all the rest. So the real value of all these separate particulars cannot be estimated alone. But when the artist begins to draw them in together, when he groups these sketches on one surface, when he blends the colors, and combines them in relation to the lights and shadows of the picture, then one may begin to see, *and not till then*, all that the studies contained. They can only be interpreted by their final combination, their place in the finished picture.

Or — to take an illustration still more analogous to the case we are seeking to make plain, because it is a part of a scheme which is never finished, but always going on — let any man of affairs undertake some large and complicated enterprise of profit, like the building of an extensive railroad line. Now, in order to make a fair judgment of the various steps of that work, it is necessary always to keep in mind its end. There are many stages in the progress of the enterprise when it seemed more like a work of demolition than one of construction. The claims upon public and private lands for location, the cutting away of forests, the digging down of hills, the rendering of property unfit for its old uses, — all these seem like undoing and depreciating and destroying. The debt, too, incurred for construction, the mortgages given on this newly made property, — is it not a thriftless use of money to put it into this highway in a wilderness? Is it wise to undertake all these risks, expend all this treasure, devote all this thought, care, anxiety? The one answer of the capitalist, of the engineer, of the managers of the scheme, is simply, "Wait and see." You must wait till you see these untenanted fields taken up by the thronging immigrants. You must wait till these streams begin to pull at the wheels of factories, these plains to turn yellow with the ripening grain, these scattering settlements to grow to hamlets and towns and thriving cities. You must wait till the heavy-laden trains toil across the country with great freights of produce, and come back bearing the supplies for these fresh communities. That is the answer to all your queries. That proves that the work was one of construction, — that it built up and increased values, and enlarged the utilities of the country. It proves that the investment was directed toward a genuine profit. It shows how well bestowed was all the thought of the financier and the builder. The purpose of that early work does not appear till late in the process of the scheme ; but when it does come, it explains and justifies everything preliminary.

Now, are not these cases quite analogous to the moral universe, or, more exactly, the universe in its moral relations? These, too, in any fair construction, must be viewed according to their issue, and not according to their temporary and transitional aspects. We must not expect the solution of these mysteries of life and being in this twilight season of our existence. We must wait " until the day break and the shadows flee away." The gospel names the only ground upon which the past and present of this weary world can be reconciled to our tolerance. " Judge nothing," says Paul, " before the time, until the Lord come." [1] Remember, he seems to say, you are beholding only a transitory and provisional state of things. The whole scheme of life centres in and takes its meaning from life's high

[1] 1 Corinthians iv. 5.

purpose. The means and the process are only to be read in the light of the achievement of the Creator's end. The whole of the long and laborious progress wrought out with such expenditure of thought, such pangs and agony, such suffering of the flesh, such anguish of spirit, is but the prelude to creation's true life, — the imparting of the life of God to His creation as fast and as far as it can receive the same, till it shall enjoy the fulness of a divine spirit in that day when the kingdoms of this world shall be subject to the will and spirit of love, — that wished-for time which men doubtfully expect in the " millennium ; " that epoch which the gospel calls " the coming of the Lord."

XII. — DIVINE FATHERHOOD AND HUMAN DESTINY.

It is upon the sublime truth of the Divine fatherhood that we build the faith in man's final holiness. Because God's nature is unalterably love, and because man's birthright is inalienably sonship, it follows that his destiny must be one of good and holiness. Upon any line of logic from this great thought, we come inevitably to the conclusion that mankind is destined to redemption from the thraldom of sin and its sequences. Justice, mercy, and love, the essential elements of fatherhood, all stand pledged to do the best for man, and to secure him from the awful destruction of an endless career of sinfulness. Once accept the truth of the Divine fatherhood in its fulness, — once realize the sublime significance that it gives to the human race, and to all the life of that race, — and it becomes impossible to doubt that God has in view a destiny of good for all His children. It is impossible to conceive of the Infinite Father as conferring life upon children, in the full knowledge that by their own acts they would make that life a curse. It is impossible to conceive of this Father as making the fate of eternity turn upon the choice of these brief earthly years. It is impossible to conceive of Him as limiting His interest in man, and his efforts for him, to the life this side the grave. It is impossible to conceive that He would turn a deaf ear to the cry for pardon which might come even from the deeps of hell. It is impossible to conceive of Him as content with any vindication of His power or any triumph of His kingdom which does not include the reconciliation of His children, and their complete recovery to the joys and the duties of their inheritance. It is impossible to conceive of any or all these things, because they are inconsistent with a fatherly character. They are utterly at variance with any conception of paternal nature which leaves that nature within the limits of our human definitions. For every human conception of fatherhood recognizes it as a relationship under law. It carries with it duties as well as privileges, — duties the highest, the noblest possible to man ; but obligations still the more sacred, as they involve these very privileges. It is understood by all enlightened minds that the father assumes a responsibility and gives a tacit pledge in the very act of becoming a parent. He is under bonds to his child. That obligation is self-imposed. He is in honor held to fulfil it.

But now we ask, is it an audacious or an unwarrantable thought of God, to say that as our Creator, as the Author of our being, He has assumed a bond, and out of His own infinite free will undertaken certain obligations to His offspring? It is not claimed that it lies in the power of man to put God under obligation. But it certainly lies in the power of God to bind

Himself. And it is only a proper tribute to
His infinite righteousness and justice, and not
in the faintest degree an irreverent assumption
of knowledge in divine things, to say that when
He created man in His own image, made him
His child and not simply His creature, gave him
a self-conscious soul, and a nature capable of the
most exquisite joy in finding its destiny as well
as the most exquisite torture in missing that end,
He put His own most adorable nature under
bonds to see to it that He secured to every one
of these conscious children of His the power to
attain that joy and avoid that terrible disaster
and loss. Set aside now every consideration in
this matter except the single one that God made
us, that He gave us all the powers that we possess, including that awful faculty, so fraught
with our own weal or woe, — the faculty of willing good or evil, — must we not say that by that
sole and separate fact the Almighty God stands,
self-bound, held by His own infinite justice and
love, to bring us to our own and lead us into life
and joy everlasting ? Righteousness must mean
the same in God as it does in man. There are
not two kinds of benevolence and of justice, of
rectitude and of love, in this universe, — one for

God and another for man. The mercy God
shows a sinner is the same in quality as that
which He enjoins upon His children. The love
He bears us is the same in kind as that we bear
each other. Else is there no meaning in the
traits we ascribe to Him, or the honor we pay to
His name. And to say that it is fair, or just, or
loving in God to endow man with a gift in whose
exercise man shall work his own eternal doom,
is to give quite other meaning to those virtues
and holy traits from what they convey when we
apply them to ourselves. It may or may not
be "an assumption unproved and unprovable"
that "God is bound by the perfections of His
nature to make all men happy;" but will any
man undertake to prove to the satisfaction of a
Christian mind and heart that it is a perfectly
fair and just procedure to endow man with a
nature so frail and peccable that it broke down
at the start, and has been working but imper-
fectly ever since, and then to doom him to eternal torments for not getting it reduced to order
and regularity during the brief years of a mortal
life? God is bound by the perfections of His
nature not to make a being whose very constitution renders it morally certain that it will be'

unhappy, not for a few brief years but forever
and forever.   To deliberately organize a soul
for a career of woe would be to lack the very
first elements of affectionate paternity.

We need not try to discover the workings of
the Infinite Mind, or attempt a psychology or a
system of ethics for Divinity. But He who
taught us to say " Our Father," and gave us the
sweet domestic thought of God which we find in
the parable of the Prodigal, surely warrants us
in thinking of Him as working in fatherly ways
and governed by motives at least as high and
loving as those that rule the hearts of earthly
fathers.   And can we think that the loving God,
knowing the awful possibilities of the life of
each separate soul, would have called us into
being unless He had foreseen that at last each
one of us would come to good and peace and joy ?
It sometimes puts a terrible strain upon our faith
in God's fatherhood to contemplate the suffering with which this earth is so full ; to see the
millions of men and women who come into this
world only to be buffeted by its adversities and
torn by its severities, dragged through its hells,
and hurried down to the dark deaths of the sinful.   And the only thought which saves us from

crying out of our sympathizing hearts that God
has made a fearful mistake in creating men is
the faith which holds us, in spite of all this misery, that God is leading man through the shadows to the stars, that strife and sorrow are
growing less, and man is being reclaimed and
fitted for a true sonship with all its joys. In
that hope one can go into the meanest hovel
where poverty grovels in rags; one can go to
the most miserable wreck of a noble life, and
say in faith, —

> " The wrong that pains my soul below
>   I dare not throne above;
> I know not of His hate, — I know
>   His goodness and His love."

But if there be no hope at the end; if God
has no alternative but to send these hapless
souls from a birth into sin, on to an eternity of
woe; if the aimless sufferings of this life are but
the prelude to sufferings in another existence
that are endless as well as aimless, — then may
we exclaim, " Would God we had never been,
rather than be and suffer all these hopeless ills!
It had been better for us that we had never been
born; better if God had left us in the silence

and the void whence we came forth; better that
we had never known the powers and the capacities of conscious life, than that, having received
them, they should be turned into a miserable and
a ceaseless curse. If God has no mercy for the
end, He might have had in the beginning."

But thanks to the revelation made in Jesus
Christ, God has vindicated His fatherly love, and
given assurance of His merciful grace, in the
pledge He has sealed to make us all alive in
Christ. He will be true to all the obligations of
fatherhood. He will leave nothing undone, no
labor and no sacrifice, to vindicate and prove
His care for His own. Once our Father he is
always our Father, and the eternal years will
not sunder nor weaken the tie that makes us
His. And that truth is the most telling, the
most persuasive, the most saving that ever was
preached to the children of men. No moral
force that ever was brought to bear upon human
life has exerted upon it such influence to save,
to regenerate, and to purify, as the truth of God's
fatherly love revealed in the sacrifice of Jesus
Christ. The ancient world was always at a loss
to find a motive which should stir men out of
their sins, and into the religious life. The world

found the missing impulse when Christ, to manifest our Father's love, came and died upon the cross. That act was at once the evidence and the illustration of the love of God. It was an object-lesson in the spiritual economy. And it touched the heart of the world. It has always touched it. It is the power which God meant should touch it. It was a revelation to man of his true spiritual birthright; and it filled him with a desire to claim his own.

XIII.—THE DIVINE FATHERHOOD AND HUMAN CONDUCT.

It is a cheering thought to him who loves this mighty truth of the Fatherhood of God, that it is just beginning to assert its power as a motive in conduct. The most intelligent and experienced workers with weak and sinful men have learned that nothing converts men, nothing wins them to God, like the simple declaration of the truth that they are God's children, partakers of His love, objects of His mercy, and capable of becoming in character what they already are in nature. There is no appeal so strong as this, none that so invariably reaches and moves the human heart.

When all other appeals to man's selfish and corrupted heart have failed, there is one thought that does not fail, and that will not fail, at last to reach every sinful soul. You may go to men with warnings, and not move them. You may hold over them the terrors of the law, and only harden them. You may appeal to their selfishness, and never rouse in them a particle of aversion to themselves and their own debased living. But many a time when all else has failed to touch human hearts, and it seems as if, for this life at least, the soul must go on its wretched and rebellious way, there is dropped some word that starts the sense of sonship, — some thought comes home to the hard heart that quickens that dead and withered feeling of relationship to God, and a claim on the blessings of the great family privileges and rights. And when that nerve is stirred it is not far away to the spot where the wanderer will meet its God in the way, and make a willing surrender to its Father. It often happens that the aged man, sick and suffering, wandering in his mind and uncertain in his memories, goes back past all the years, and seems to be living again the years of his boyhood. He is once more a child in the old home. He calls the names of his play-mates. He wanders in the old haunts, roams the old fields, plays the old games. He has lost all hold upon the years, be they good or be they bad, which lie between him and those early days. Everything else has slipped away from him. But the one thing which memory will not let go is the thought of childhood, the ties which knit themselves there, and the loves formed then, which have lasted through all the long years of labor and of loss. And so when a human soul lies in the weakness and exhaustion of its life-long sins, and is insensible to every call that would rouse it from the stupor of degradation, there is one voice, one summons, which seems to set all the heartstrings in motion, and to reach the one instinct which cannot be removed from the soul, of sonship to God.

And what follows when this perception of the eternal relationship is once aroused in the heart? What are the consequences of a recognition of God's fatherhood and our sonship? There are two faces to this truth; and while the one looks toward God, there is another and equally mo-mentous one which looks directly at us. We need have no fear but that through all eternity our Father will be true to His obligations, per-

form every duty and guard every interest of His
children. We are safe in His hands, and we
have nothing to fear from Him. For whether
He smite or whether He heal, whether He act
or whether He wait; whether He come to us
with tenderness or in the fire of His wrath, " He
doeth all things well." He is eternally true to
His fatherhood.

But are we as faithful to our sonship? Do we
serve God as faithfully as God serves us? Do
we give as He gives? God acknowledges His relationship to us. But do we, even while we feel
and believe that we bear God's image, rise to the
height of the duties which that fact lays upon
every one of us? Every truth has an ethical
bearing. Some duty grows out of every fact of
the moral nature. And the most imperative, the
most exacting, the most sweeping truth in its relation to the human conscience, is that of man's
sonship to God. What does a child owe to a parent? What does dependence owe to the strength
on which it hangs? What does feebleness owe
to the care which nurses it, and ignorance to
the wisdom which guides and instructs, and
waywardness to the heart that restrains and
chastens? What does helplessness owe to love?
What does the transgressor owe to the heart

of mercy and of pardon? That, all that and more, man owes to his Father. We cannot read that fact of the spiritual world and shut our eyes to its personal import. The light that streams from it illuminates conscience as well as intellect; it reveals a duty as well as a hope. You are a son of God; but are you living like one? You belong to the great family; but have you done your duty by your brother, or your father? You are entitled to your inheritance as an heir of life; have you ever claimed your own? You are debtor to the Father, who begot you, reared you, endowed you, educated you, and still holds your portion in trust for you; have you ever paid a farthing of your debt, by gratitude, by the giving of your love in return, by obedience, or by sacrifice?

There is no humiliation in this life more complete than that which overtakes the man who finds he has been unjust to his friend; has repaid love with suspicion, benefits with coldness, and generous interest with aversion. When the blinded and perverse heart sees what it has done, it bends in the heaviness of grief and of mortification. One does not like to look into the face which has been thus repelled, and feel that

life has been one long, sad mistake. And worst
of all is the shame which befalls when the one
who has been wronged is a father, who has been
robbed of filial tenderness, cheated of that love
which was his due, kept out of the sympathy and
appreciative recognition which is the best re-
ward of his heart for all its denials and its
labors. Can we imagine any remorse more cutting. than that which pierces the heart of him
who has been a false, a hard, a wayward son,
coming at last to a consciousness of his crime?
And yet that, and worse, is the fate of every soul
which forgets its duties to the Heavenly Father,
turns its back on God, and cheats Him of the
honor and the love which is His due. For our
disobedience is robbery from God. Estranged
from Him, we wrong His love; and when we
come to ourselves, it is to find that we have been
sinning against our dearest Friend. Thank God,
He has forgiveness for even this wrong, and
when we turn us again to His face, He meets
with outstretched arms His returning sons and
daughters.

University Press : John Wilson & Son, Cambridge.

www.ingramcontent.com/pod-product-compliance
Lightning Source LLC
Chambersburg PA
CBHW021409090426
42742CB00009B/1075